THE BEAUTY

I0142753

OF BUSINESS

7 Simple Ways to Captivate, Convert & Build Your Brand Identity

Audrey L. Woodley, B.S., M.A.

The Brand Therapist

7 Simple Ways to Captivate, Convert & Build Your Brand Identity

Better Destination Media Book

BDM, Inc. Publishing, Chicago

Disclaimer

www.audreywoodley.com

TABLE OF CONTENTS

CHAPTER ONE

FROM THE CLASSROOM TO THE STAGE

Entrepreneurship isn't for everyone, you must have a drive and commitment to stick with it, even when the money isn't coming in, or the credit card you swipe is declined. Growing your business has to do with time and patience, but there is a reward when you stay focused on your dreams and never give up.

The thought of being my own boss and running my own company, has always been on my mind ever since I was a little girl. My mother and my grandmother made sure that I was in school, getting a great education. So after graduating from college, I got my first job as an 8th grade math teacher at the Houston Independent School District.

Even though teaching was my first passion, I also loved shopping. Working in retail cured my shopping habits, and that was all I needed. Just more clothes to dress up and feel beautiful. My two favorite jobs were at Bloomingdale's and Nordstrom. I had a ball working at these two department stores, and as a matter of fact Nordstrom has become one of The Beauty of Business partners. Because this is where I developed the skill of building customer relationships, and how to sell items. I realized I love working to help others look good, and with the experience and passion. I opened my first second-hand store on the west side of Chicago, while I still maintained my teaching job. This was the beginning of my journey of building a business that teaches women how to build their own businesses and brands.

My college education did come with a road map, but my entrepreneurship journey didn't. When I started looking for programs and mentors to help me build my not-for-profit organization, there were none available in my area. However, with my networking skills, I used my proficiency in online research and networking events to find professional women and men who had the expertise to help me understand my gifts, and how to deliver it to the marketplace. Many people were claiming to be coaches, and charging overrated prices, and that actually put me in the hole at the beginning. They had no prior coaching experience, but I was willing to take the risk to get my feet wet in the coaching business. Although, I had the problem of not trusting myself and lacked the confidence in growing my business. But in the midst of it all, quitting has never been a part of my vocabulary, so I continued to pray and ask God for direction for my business.

After working for years teaching in the classroom, I began to feel like the walls were closing in on me, and I wanted more out of my life and career. Well, it happened to me, I got the "pink slip," I was totally caught off guard. I thought I was going to leave when I got good and ready. So, just as I was looking to start my entrepreneurship journey, I got an email from an old friend of mine. I must say, that was my first opportunity to get my feet into hosting and speaking at different events. Since, becoming Amazon Best Selling Author, "Network, to Increase Net Worth," since then I've been able to collaborate, and work with other leaders on several other book joint venture projects and also created my own lane.

Creating a market for your niche comes with you being able to identify your gift and talent and how to position your story to connect to your ideal audience. However, building my brand still didn't give me the return on my dollars, so that you know you still have to create your niche even if they don't come. Stay focused, and trust the process. Don't let your dreams die but have the mindset that your dreams will manifest. You have to create a balance and work with coaches that align with your vision. All coaches are not created equal, some coaches see

www.audreywoodley.com

5

you as a dollar sign, and some coaches see you like a flower that they want to nurture and grow. Here are a few things you need to do before you hire a coach. The first thing that you would need to do is sign up for an email, join their group, or listen to their podcast. Take a few of their programs that fit into your budget before investing your whole check away. Hint: coaches have you sign a contract and it's important you read the terms. Most coaches have a cancellation policy to pay, even if you do decide to cancel. Now you have just lost your passion for starting the business and money that you've just invested, you're not getting back.

 The Journey of becoming an entrepreneur is not for the quitters, you must study and understand that each road leads you to a bigger destination. Even though I paid for coaching and programs, there is nothing more refreshing than taking what you paid for and putting it into action.

Creating a book tor and partnering with brands like Nordstrom, Henri Bendel, MAC, and Lord & Taylor along with my vision, I created my own panel speakers in three years with the black Women's Expo, which has given me more experience and leadership skills to create what is today known as 'The Brand Launch Society.' The BLS was created to help women launch their own product, service, or event without the cost of jumping from coach to coach or losing money and time in the process, which leads to a bigger headache. My goal is to coach self-confidence, believing in yourself and empowering women to step out and manifest their dreams into building a system that creates a sustainable income where they can travel or buy the luxury car they want.

2018 Black Women Expo, Moderator & Speaker

Creating a name for myself and my business was the greatest gift that I rewarded myself with. As, you can tell it came with a lot of bumps and valleys, but you can overcome anything if you have a desire to win and be a piece of the puzzle to help someone with their dreams. I've taken all of my experience from retail, teaching, and starting my own companies into thorough account to help women start their own business. The gift of understanding your niche is a perfect example of where you can live a life of freedom and enjoy the things that the world has to offer you.

For every experience in life whether good or bad, is a real-life lesson learned. You can always go back and learn something different. Let your failures be your success!

Audrey Woodley is a Brand Therapist who helps women identify solutions to their brand challenges. She uses new-age problem solving tactics, with proven strategies and customized solutions to help women build and sustain a successful brand.

www.audreywoodley.com

CHAPTER TWO

WHAT'S YOUR WHY?

Building your personal brand and identity has never been easier or more important than it is today.

EVERYONE - needs to start thinking of themselves as a brand. It is no longer an option; it is a necessity."- says Gary Vaynerchuk.

Your brand marketing strategy is what allows you to distinguish yourself from everyone else, and make yourself memorable. It allows you to attract your ideal clients - clients who understand and connect with you.

What is branding?

There are 3 key components to your brand. They are what I call the "3 W's".

1. WHO - your target market or who you are trying to attract.

2. WHAT - the specific problem you help your target market solve, and the results you help them achieve.

1 and 2 combined are your niche definition. You have to get really clear on your niche if you are going to create a successful brand.

Many entrepreneurs struggle with finding their niche, but it's the foundation of your business success. Finding your niche is based on much more than keyword research. It involves tapping into your passions, skills, experiences and interests. It means understanding the challenges and needs of your target market. And it requires you investing into research about your niche to make sure you have clarity and focus.

3. WHY - the third part of your personal brand is your WHY and it includes: Why you do what you do? And Why people should work with you?

This is your opportunity to share your personal story and your passion for what you do. It is your chance to put a memorable face on your business. Branding is much more than a logo or tag line. It is the heart and soul of your business.

Take the time to identify your ideal niche, and from there create a personal brand that is authentic to who you are.

What is your core concept? It's your BIG idea, the central thought that everything else is built on. In story writing we call it your theme. It's the kernel of truth that becomes the strong foundation for your work. What special takeaway or benefits do you offer your clients? And, what happens when you add value to someone's life; it's like dropping a pebble into a pond. The effects ripple's outward. Find the benefit from the last ripple your service creates, then you're on to your core concept.

Remember these 3 points about your core concept:

1. It has to be real.

Your promise must precisely match the results. Be careful about making over-rated promises, and also about under-rated promises. When you are authentic, the results are real and your Perfect Prospect feels it.

2. It has to be exciting.

What's the most thrilling part of your service, the thing that makes your clients breathe, "Wow!" Does that particular benefit fall dead center to your core concept? If it does, use this electrifying moment as your focal point. It will stir the imagination and curiosity of your Perfect Prospect and draw them in.

3. It has to be too good to keep.

Does the answer to #2 stir up an urgency to call Mom or share on Facebook? That's what you're looking for. News that's too good to keep will spur your business into the stratosphere with viral marketing. That's the sweet spot you've been searching for.

If you're an interior designer whose focus is on senior living, then your theme could be, "I'll design a custom living space so you can enjoy the comfort and security of your home for years to come." That's a real, valid claim. It's exciting to people facing the hard choices in life and it's something to share with friends and family members facing the same challenges.

Once you have your core concept down, stick to it. Everything has to revolve around that one message. In a story, every single scene, every single conversation, every single incident must be tied to the theme and to the storyline. Yes, you might get a cute idea for a conversation or situation between 2 of the characters but unless that incident is vital to the theme, it has to go.

The same is true of your business theme. Every single product you offer, every single teleseminar and report must stick to the theme as well. Keep your message pure. Just keep driving that message home, so you become known for that single concept. Become an authority in that precise piece of real estate although you can come at the theme in a lot of different ways. With one strong theme, you can create an entire 7-figure industry. Lisa Nichols did, Tony Robbins and Jack Canfield did, Oprah did, so can you.

Your theme should automatically lead to a call to action. Once you know your theme, you'll present it in a way that naturally leads your prospects to the next step. Yes, your prospects want to build a blog that will help them connect to their tribe on a soul level. So, how will they get that benefit? By engaging with you and getting the help you (the best authority) can give them.

Once you understand the values and the pain of your Perfect Prospects, you will know how to frame your theme, your products, and your call to action. What do your prospects want? Legacy? Security? Health and wellness for their loved ones? By expanding on your theme, you will touch them at the deepest levels. Yes, they want to have a great lifestyle, but what will that do for them? When you mention the final ripple, you will get their attention. They will move for the mouse and the buy now button.

Can you see how this comes down to knowing who your prospects are and what they need from you? If you know that, then you can deliver exactly what they need every single time. You can craft your products and services, then talk about them using the very words that captures their attention and you'll knock it out of the park every time.

Brand Story

The brand story and pitching can be very challenging when starting out, so I created a webinar and a worksheet to help you get clear with your personal story and statement. This will help you get clear about your Why; so you can start building your brand authority online. As part of the Brand Launch Society membership program, helping entrepreneurs ease this part plus giving them a clear direction on how to position themselves with their pitch and how to create their avatar profile.

We also created the Brand Story Challenge to help coaches and self-published authors to understand how crucial it is to know your story, plus how to connect with the audience as well as getting paid to speak and sponsorships.

Example:

I wanted to connect with a niche market and give them an unforgettable experience, so I created something that was dear to me and by creating a legacy to where I give honor to my mother, who is a ten year breast cancer survivor which I host an Annual Legacy Brunch every year with Beauty For A Cause. The beauty of my brand story and pitching to sponsors help to leverage more speaking engagements and credibility for my brands.

Start your brand story challenge today, click to get started here…..bit.ly/Brand2Top

CHAPTER THREE

THE BUSINESS MAP

Building your personal or business brand is no accident, you are building a legacy for your future self, so don't take it lightly when people ask you, what do you do? It's a crowded market, and you have to be unique, when people come knocking on your door. One of the reasons why they will be knocking on your door, is because you have a Signature Program and business model that is solving your client's problem, and they are sharing the good news. In this chapter you will start to bring your "A" game. Most business can't live without a business model or marketing plan, most coaches will ask you for this, so you might as well be prepared. Note (please be sure to survey and test the model to your hot leads before casting the big net).

To give you a little insight, you can look up business canvas model in your Android Apps, it gives you the layout, but for the sake of this book, we want to help you stay right here.

The first thing is going back to your brand story, what is your clients problem? You might have the solution to their problem. For example my ideal client's problem is visibility, systems, and marketing. So, how can my products/services help with all three of these issues. So, I came up with the three solutions that I have experienced in my business and created my own Signature Program called: Brand Launch Society, a three month accelerated business program that teaches women how to create a business plan, Signature Model & Systems, and launch it to their customers.

Next, what is your USP? Unique Value Proposition, and how are you different from others? Again, we can go back to our brand story, where we have the three things that needs to happen and hoe to make it a part of your story.

Example USP: I coach high-level achievers, take inventory, and detox what's not working. Later I create a personal business strategy map that will transform their money story, credibility, brand visibility and business tools that will give them confidence, and convert sales. As a result of working with me, clients has increased engagement and sales by 25%.

For marketing purposes, you have to understand what channels you will be engaging with them and what segments will you be able to connect with your audience and be present.

Now, you have just about everything except for the money. Oh yeah! The money, the first thing that all business women need to understand is that this business needs to make money, and you have to structure into your business and create revenue streams that will keep the business going. If you don't plan, you plan to fail", women don't know their value, and they don't have a clue on how to position themselves as the thought leader, which means they're leaving money on the table. So, let's work through one revenue stream, and I will choose coaching. Let's say my goal is to make $5k a month and, I'm only working with 3 people. So, you will come out to about charging about $1666 per client. You will have to structure your programs and online systems to meet your clients need. Your customers are looking for coaches that are serving on a high level, but this is one way on how to design your cost structure. Nothing is set in stone, but you have to be able to know your sweet spot and use a strategic business model to help you stay focused on meeting your financial goals.

Next, your business model must be translated into a sales page or lead magnet that your clients can connect or use in helping them solve their problem. See examples below:

You can begin by checking out the examples of my *business model canvas,* and you will begin to see that my goal was to create the Brand Launch Society (Program Name).

Customer Segments- target market (use your USP, to distribute through these channels).

1. Mass Market

2. Niche Market

3. Segmented

Value Propositions- Work with these ideas to begin to understand your USP.

1. Connect with your friends, discover your unique talents, and express the benefits.

2. What values do you deliver to the customer?

3. Which one of your customer's problems are you helping to solve?

4. What bundles of products and services are you offering to each customer?

Developing strong value propositions does not only makes it easier to connect with target audiences, but it establishes a foundation upon which a company's marketing and sales activities can be built upon.

Channels- What's cost effective, which is the best channel, and how am I reaching them now, and am I integrating them with customer routine?

1. Blogs/Podcast/Insta Stories

2. Facebook Groups

3. Facebook Ads

4. Facebook Business Pages

5. Instagram Ads

6. Google Ads

7. Business Funnel

Customer Relationships

What type of relations does each customer segment expect us to establish and maintain with them, and how much is it costing us?

Key Activities:

What Key Activities do your VP requires, what are your distribution channels, Customer Relationships? Revenue Streams?

Key Solutions- Visibility, Systems, Campaign Launches

1. Branding

2. Signature Offer

3. Sales page with CRM Integration

4 Content Marketing Creation

5. Livestream

Key Metrics- This is the lifeline of your business. There are nine key metrics

1. Customer Acquisition Costs (CAC)

2. Customer Retention

3. Attrition

4. Life-Time Value

5. Product Metabolism

6. Viral Coefficient

7. Revenue

8. Conversation Rate

9. Referral Rate

Cost Structure -

What value are your customers really willing to pay?

For what do they currently pay?

How much are they currently paying?

How much would they prefer to pay?

How much does each Revenue Stream contribute to overall revenues?

Revenue Stream -

How are you creating your Signature Product to make multiple streams of income? Once you create your Signature Product, you can create a model from that success and create a membership program, book joint venture, get paid to speak, etc... The most important of this is for you to understand what stage you are in your business and create or design products that will solve your client's problem.

SWOT- what are your strengths, weakness, opportunities, and threats.

Starting a business in this digital tech age can be very difficult. So in order to make the right decisions, you must have the information to make better decision and predictable income for your business. You have all the access to your business, all you need to know is what to pay attention to.

Start looking at the data and know if you are spending to much time in one area that is not making any money. Look at your marketing strategy and see what you can adjust to create a revenue stream that is duplicatable.

Make sure you download a copy of the business model template and do a better testing of your product before you break the bank.

You can use the template below to complete your business model for your brand development and business launch.

Key Partners	Key Activities	Value Propositions	Customer Relationships	Customer Segments
	Key Resources		Channels	

Cost Structure	Revenue Streams

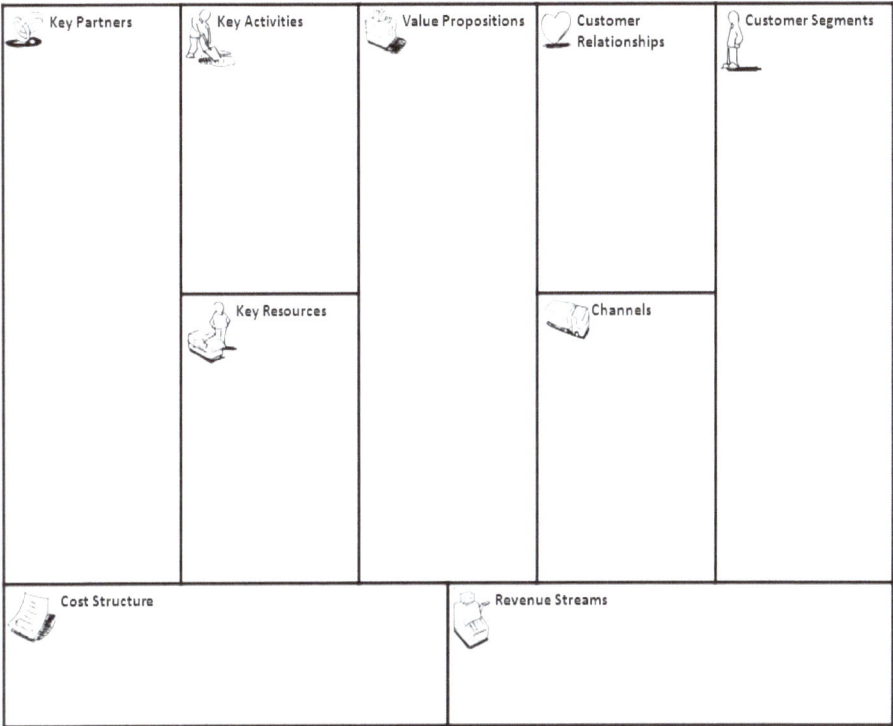

For more support on getting your business map started, book your call here bit.ly/B2BTherapy

CHAPTER FOUR

THE SIGNATURE PRODUCT

The Brand Launch Society class will help you boost your confidence so that you attain greater heights in your business. Confidence is a great determinant that contributes immensely to the performance of every business.

The Brand Launch Society Application form is to screen all interested business women or men that are interested in building a speaking platform and a strategic partnership. The Brand Launch Society Summit, JV Book Launch & Beauty For A Cause Signature Event, are three Signature Events.. The Summit will launch 2019 & Book Launch March 2019 at our Annual Retreat. This is an investment opportunity with high level achievers who are ready to advance their business and personal brand with our Signature System & Coaching by Audrey Woodley & Team.

Our Mission- Claim Your Space it's Your Time!

We're interviewing women that are ready to STEP IT UP. My acclaimed accelerated 6 month coaching program. Branding, Marketing, Content Mapping, Sales, Client Attraction, Campaign Building, & Entrepreneurship.

The Mood Board Guide

Your brand identity and what you deliver helps set you apart from your competition. Design your marketing and media kit to make a connection with potential influencers or sponsors that align with my brand's

www.audreywoodley.com

mission. Your brand logo, font, imagery, voice, story, and pitch are just a few things to help you get started on creating your brand awareness.

Please find enclosed links workbook and let's get together for your next launch. In the meantime, we have the 5 Day Workflow & Systems Boot Camp. {bit.ly/Brand2Top}

to help you save time and scale your business and create more revenue.

Click & Download the personal brand discovery workbook.

>>>>>>>>>>http://bit.ly/AchieveJournal<<<<<<<<<<

Your brand is an extension of you offline and keeping the conversations going with your ideal audience. Have your graphic designer create you a brand style guide or use CANVA if you have the skills. Your brand should consist of your colors, imagery, font, and logo. You can use your style guide to develop your persona and the message you want to get across to your clients on your social media platforms. Your brand messaging, pictures, and the opt-in system is key to building your brand.

To connect and build relationships with future sponsors, I pitch an introductory email along with a 2 page sponsorship kit to show my social media presence on pages 23 & 24. On page 25, I created an opt-in email lead magnet to register for the 7 Boss Move, Captivate & Convert Ebook launch.

Audrey Woodley

AMBASSADOR BLOGGER & AUTHOR

about the blogger

Audrey Woodley is Brand Therapist who helps women identify solutions to their brand challenges. She uses new-age problem solving tactics. proven strategies and customized solutions to help women build and sustain a successful brand. Launched Better Destination Media, Social Media & Marketing Boutique for Speakers, Authors, & Coaches.

about the blog

The blog focuses on personal development, branding, and business strategies for women creating an online business. Along with the blog we host quarterly interviews with stylist and bloggers to keep our community engaged and build brand loyalty with out fan base.
Monthly page views 10k+

statistics

f	t	o	p
500,00+	5k	3K	10k+

773-309-1047 · info@audreywoodley.com · @audreywoodley

www.audreywoodley.com

services offered

Styling for photoshoots (editorials, publications, advertising, music videos, fashion films, personal etc.)

Brand Ambassador Training/MySuitMe

Personal shoppers/ Stylists (Once-off, temps or permanent services)

Event Planning

Integrated Marketing

Lord & Taylor

You're invited!

HENRI BENDEL

Enjoy

25% OFF

SUNDAY, OCTOBER 16TH
4.00PM–6.00PM

HENRI BENDEL
NEW YORK

collaboration bae

Package A: $500

A package of information assembled by a Better Destination Media, Inc. to provide basic information about the client to reporters.

Package B: $300

A package of information assembled by a Better Destination Media, Inc. to provide basic information about the client to sponsors.

contact details

Address

2352 W. Warren Blvd
Chicago, Il 60612

Phone / Email

777.309.1047 / info@;audreylwoodley.com

Website / Social Media

www.audreywoodley.com / @audreywoodley

HENRI BENDEL
NEW YORK

www.audreywoodley.com

7 BOLD BRAND MOVES CHECKLIST

THE BRAND
THERAPIST

DOMAIN/WEBSITE
SECURE YOUR BRAND

BlueHost
WordPress
SqaureSpace
GoodDaddy

BRAND/GRAPHICS
BUILD YOUR BRAND IDENTITY

Logo/brand colors/font
Deposit Photos
Design Pickle

Build Audience
KNOW YOUR IDEAL CLENTS NEEDS

Create Your Podcast
Take survey of clients needs
Pick two platforms to build engagement

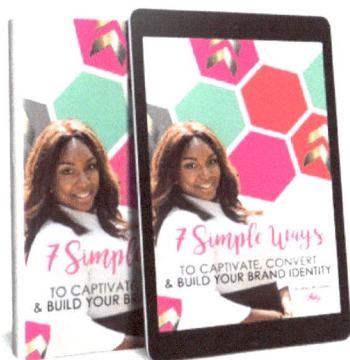

List Builders
TURN FANS INTO PAYING CLIENTS

Active Campaign
Mailcimp
Convertkit

"DON'T WAIT FOR OPPORTUNITIES, CREATE THEM"

www.audreywoodley.com

CHAPTER FIVE

SECURE YOUR PARTNERSHIP

There's no standard way to create success in your business or personal life. Each woman has her own success formula. One thing that many successful women have in common is; Building Strategic Partnerships. Strategic partnerships are extremely beneficial when it comes to business growth, personal growth, and success. Sure, you can reach a level of success on your own, but the journey will be much longer and unnecessarily tougher. True success requires input from multiple people; the saying still holds true "it's not what you know, but who you know." Building relationships and partnerships with the right people can take you to higher levels of success. As a business owner for more than 10 years, I can attest to the power of strategic partnerships, and how I've successfully grown my business through strategic partnerships. Building partnerships requires patience, trust, and clearly defined goals. Here are the 5 steps I have used in securing strategic partnerships:

Step 1: Find the common bond: I've had many partnerships, some successful and some unsuccessful. What I've learned in order to make a partnership successful is finding a common bond. When looking for your next potential partner it's important to identify what common bond you and the partner share.

Step 2: Make it Mutually Beneficial: Once you've identified the common bond, the next step is to make the partnership mutually beneficial. This is the core of what makes a partnership valuable. An ideal partnership equally benefits both partners.

Step 3: Make the Pitch: Now that you've identified the common bond and made sure the partnership is equally beneficial, now it's time to pitch the partnership. When pitching your partnership idea, be clear on what you want in the said partnership and what you're willing to give. A tactic I have applied when pitching is leveraging previous successful partnerships and showcasing the results.

Step 4: Be Open to Partnering in Non-Traditional Ways: Sometimes partnerships grows into full-scale business, lifelong friendships, or unexpected wins. For instance, during one of my recent partnerships, I was gifted a luxury backpack, a surprising win that came from a successful partnership. When thinking about your next partnership, try to stay open to partnering in non-traditional ways.

Step 5: Host An Event Together: Events are key to building brand awareness, networking, and finding customer leads. With today's technology you can host an event with your partner and be in separate cities, online events through social media, webinars, and teleconferences make great partnership event ideas. Once you've worked out all the details of your partnership, hosting an event together is a great way to elevate your brand, cut cost, and reach a broader audience.

You're invited!
Please join Audrey for a private night
of Sips and Shopping at

HENRI BENDEL

Enjoy

25% OFF

New Arrivals

SUNDAY, OCTOBER 16TH
4:00PM–6:00PM

HENRI BENDEL, WATER TOWER PLACE
845 MICHIGAN AVENUE, CHICAGO, IL

HENRI BENDEL
NEW YORK

CHAPTER SIX

HOW TO SCALE BUSINESS FOR SUCCESS

Is it possible to make your business bigger than just you? What do you have to do to grow a business веyond the founder?

I am not talking about dry skin here. What I am talking about is, does your business have capability beyond what you do personally? Is your business more than just you?

Have you built a business that can easily grow? This is a challenge for the one or two person business. If all or most of the sales of the business are based on the effort of the owner, then your business does not have scale, as of yet.

How can you change this? The approach would be to look at expanding your products, your services or your geographic reach beyond what you can do on your own. If you are running one store, consider opening another. Tim Horton's started with one! Can you develop products from the services you offer so that you increase your revenue? Brain storm around what products you might be able to sell, and consider selling digitally. Can you create reports, checklists or books?

How much income can your business make if the founder is not involved? We are all looking for passive income, income you can earn in your pajamas. If you make your money by selling your time, as many of us do, then you only have so much time to sell, and you can likely only get so much for each hour. In order to grow your business you have to get beyond selling your time. This is an area where your website will help. Is your website just a brochure for your business? Can you change that so that your website can sell products for you, and deliver these products all on its own?

What if you had more people's time to sell? If you are able to obtain more work than you can do personally, it is time to hire more employees. You can be more profitable if you can hire people to do some of the work that you do and this will free up some of your time to do more profitable work.

Can you picture yourself with more employees? If not why not? Is it possible that what is holding your business back from growth is your own limiting beliefs? Get rid of negative 'mindset.' Maybe you could scale your business by visualization which is picturing yourself actually doing it. Imagine your business with 10 more employees or a number of new locations. What would you need to do to make that happen?

If your business is the size that which you are comfortable with, then you do not care if it scales, enjoy things just the way they are.

WHAT TO CONSIDER WHEN SCALING YOUR BUSINESS

What you should keep in mind when deciding to grow your business is that regardless of your background in business or what you are offering consumers, beginning a new business is a very risky venture. Statistics show that almost 90 percent of all start-ups fail, and of that 90 percent, roughly three out of four companies failed because they decided to scale up too quickly or too soon. While this may seem like a bleak outlook, the good news is that premature business scaling is completely preventable.

Here are some things to keep in mind when scaling your business model.

Consider the State of Your Industry Over the Next Few Years

The state of your industry has a lot more to do with the success of your business than you may believe. Before scaling your business model, consider what the state of the industry may be over the next three, five, or even ten years. Will the industry be able to support the growth of your business? Will you be able to see some profit before the product or service you are offering becomes obsolete? These, among others, are important questions you need to ask yourself before beginning your business growth.

Make Sure Every Aspect of Your Business is Scalable

Many small business owners believe that scaling their business is as simple as acquiring more customers and more sales while still using their same business operations. It is important to keep in mind that true scaling usually involves several overhauls of both your business's internal and external operations. Do you have recruitment processes in place to hire more employees to support the demand? Will the technology your business currently uses support a higher workload of increased transactions, accounts, and customers? Scaling your business is more than just selling more of what you are offering.

Think About Your Business Culture

When you scale your business, you will often have to hire more employees in order to support the larger operation. Many small business owners are used to working in small groups, usually less than ten employees, and often do not understand how the business culture and dynamic will change with a larger group of employees working together toward a common goal. When your business begins to grow, focusing on your company's culture will become very important.

Some questions you may want to consider include: "What is your company's culture now?" "What kind of culture do you want your business to have?" "How will you focus on managing, and growing the company culture you desire?" By documenting best practices and guidelines from others, it will be possible to grow and nurture a culture that will work for your business as well as helping to formalize your strategic ideals, company mission, and other aspects of your growing business.

Keep Short Term and Long Term Goals in Balance

An important part of beginning and sustaining growth is making sure your goals are in balance. Investing in new technology, and/or a new business infrastructure is a short term goal that can help to lead to longer term growth. But, working toward a long term goal will likely put the shorter term goals on hold. It is important to keep the long-term impacts to your business and the short term achievements toward traction. It is vital for business growth and can often be more of an art than a science.

You have to understand that the strategies that grow your business do not have to be complicated to be effective.

To grow your business and bring in the money, turning to complicated new marketing ninja moves may not be the best move to make. Sometimes, just creating or changing the systems you already have in your business, can add a lot of extra cash that you may be leaving on the table.

Here are 14 actions and strategies that can grow your business and put more money in your bank account which you may not have considered.

1. Be Fanatical About Service & quality

When clients are talking about you and your service, most of the time, they talk about how they were treated in your business before they talk about the results you created for them. If you're fanatical about the quality of service that you offer, your clients will become the referral machines you want them to be.

We all like people that care, courteous and considerate to us. Those are the people we tend to gravitate to when we have a problem that needs solving even though they may not be the cheapest out there for the service being provided.

2. Have a Sustainable Unique Selling Proposition

Who is it that cares about what you are doing? And why should they care? Make a decision to continually establish your reason for being in business to your audience. What is it that will make you stand out from the crowd? - do you offer better value for money, or quicker service, more reliable, better quality, friendlier?

Pick what it is that makes you stand out and add that to the results that you get for your clients to build your sustainable USP. Then go out there and make noise about it.

3. Creatively Imitate Your Competition

What is it that makes your competition stand out? What can you learn from them? Is there anything you can learn from them about how they attract clients which you can incorporate into your systems to be the same?

4. Educate Your Customer

Sometimes, your customer may not know about the benefits that you're actually offering. You may actually be focusing on the features of your service. Get clear on the benefits you offer.

What is the end result that you actually get when clients work with you? What is that tangible thing they get from you after parting with their hard earned cash?

If your clients do not know what this is, they will most often be reluctant to spend any more money with you, because they cannot immediately see the value that you offer. FOCUS on your benefits - you help them lose weight faster, you help them make more money, you save them time etc.

5. Manage Your Current Activities

Sometimes, it's not the new marketing ninja move that brings in the gold mine. It's the tried and tested method that you may be neglecting. Look back at your business, is there anything you did in the past that brought clients through the door? If there is, aim to scale that activity up, and spread it as far wide as possible rather than trying to master some other new move.

If guest blogging brought clients to your website and you got clients out of that, can you find 20 great blogs that you can send in a guest post for?

If interviews are your thing, can you find 20 places you can do interviews for? If gift vouchers are your thing, can you find 20 or more sources that you can distribute your gift vouchers to? It's all about increasing the scale of what has brought success in the past.

6. Handle Objections To Close The Deal

When clients object: "we can't afford it, it won't work for me, don't need it just yet etc" - they are actually interested in your service, but just need reassurance that your service will do what you say it will do. An objection is actually a request for more information.

As long as your customers are objecting, you are selling. Until the customer disappears, then you have possibly lost the sale. Learn how to pre-empt the most common objections that clients tend to have with your business and you will book more clients.

7. Practice Price Discrimination

Different customers have different perceptions of price and how much to spend on a product or service. Offering different products to cover different price points allows you to reach a wider audience of your market and it also stops the discount requests in its tracks.

8. Ask For Referrals

Sometimes, the easiest way to bring in more money into your business is to work with someone who has come from a referral. They already know what you can do because they have seen the results from their friends, whom have worked with you, so you don't have to start from scratch to sell to them. They are already willing to buy from you. Set up systems that make it easy for your past clients to refer your business.

9: Follow Up

Just because a prospect did not immediately buy from you, does not mean they will not ever buy from you. Sometimes they just need more information. Sometimes they just need continuous reminder: "Hi, just checking in to see if you required more information, Is Tuesday a good time for us to arrange a phone meet about moving forward with this?" -

Don't be afraid to follow up and then ask for the sale. They are expecting you to do that at some point. You just have to find a way to do it that is authentic to you. But do it, you must.

10. Offer Payment Plans

Offering different ways of payment increases the income that you'll have coming into your business. Not everyone will be able to pay the full fees at once. An installment plan makes it easier for more customers to come on board.

11. Reverse The Risk

Have you considered offering 100 percent money back guarantee on your service? I think this one explains itself. If people know they can get their money back if the service does not do what you say it will do, then they will be more willing to buy from you.

12. Are You Cross Selling?

Hair Salons & Spas do this so well. You go in for a blow dry or a facial and come out with a bag full of expensive shampoo, conditioners and some other stuff that will keep your hair silky smooth or stuff that will keep your skin smooth and blemish free.

13. Are You Up-Selling?

Every online business should have this strategy like their arsenal. How this could work in an online business is to have some sort of a membership program or paid forum that you can up sell your clients to, from the eBook or one time service you have provided. A forum or membership site gives continued support from where your one-time service left off.

14. Have you Considered Joint Ventures?

We're not experts at everything. Putting your expertise together with someone who is an expert at something else to create a product, is a great way of adding income into your business.

Conclusion:

There are so many other ways that you can grow your business and make more money without necessarily having to spend more money. Most of the strategies I've mentioned here only require a bit more of your time rather than money, and even at that, if you set up your systems in your business properly, you'll find that most of them will be automated and not require a lot of time but will still bring in results.

YOUR TO-DO TASK:

1. Pick one action - just one and IMPLEMENT IT!

Consistent action is what creates results. You don't have to do everything at once (that's just crazy) but if you commit to just one action or strategy at a time, you'll be amazed at the changes you can create in your business profits.

What if you just can't get those clients through the door? It can be by trying to get clients consistently into your small business, but if you do not know what you really need to do in order to get the job done. But you want to really start getting more clients and customers in your business, well you'll need to learn a few strategies that work amazingly well.

CHAPTER SEVEN

HOW TO CAPTIVATE TO CONVERT

It is already tough enough putting in the work to become an entrepreneur; it is even tougher capturing the attention of your target market. With so many impeding factors such as competition, technology and finances; it is more difficult to be prominently positioned in the consumers' minds. There is so much information that can be instantly gathered, but with so many competitors in every direction, which makes it difficult to gain a firm grasp on the marketplace. In order to gain attention and standout, you have to embrace the needs of the consumers and make them feel valued. You have to make business an enlightening experience, yes difficult but it can be achieved with the right ingredients.

The question many will ask is, "How do I captivate the consumers and enlighten their experience with my business?" It can be difficult to make someone feel happy about paying for something like taxes, medical visits and lawyer consultation but it can be achieved. The task at hand is to make the process enjoyable through a consumer oriented business model. This is very important due to the fact that consumers now hold the power within the marketplace. With so many options available for consumers to choose from to do business at, it creates a very competitive and demanding marketplace to function within. Businesses have to be aware of this fact and act according to the environment. There is limited opportunity to under achieve the consumers' expectations, which means excellence has to be a consistent factor within your customer relationship management strategy.

Let's Identify How To Captivate And Convert Excellence To The Consumers:

7 Incredibly Powerful Tips to Captivate and Convert Massive Amounts of Sales From Your Advertising

Tip #1 - The MOST Important Decision

Now, before I tell you this one, I want you to know that if you don't remember anything else from these tips, remember this one (of course, if you really like this one, keep reading and combine it with the rest for best results)!

The single most important decision in your advertising and quite possibly your business is How you position your product.

I'll say that again.

The single most important decision in your advertising and quite possibly your business is How you position your product.

For example, if I were in business to sell toothpaste, would I want to position it to sell as a product that gets teeth really clean or a product that is good for people with sensitive teeth?

Or another example, if I were selling smartphones, would I want to position to sell to the everyday person or to the tech-savvy person?

While these are just examples to get you thinking, it is extremely important of you to know that the decision of how you position your product is a decision you must make before any advertising. Doing so will put you at a significant advantage.

If nothing else, at least give this one a try and see for yourself.

Think about how you want to position yourself and make that decision.

Tip #2 - A Large Promise

Next up is also a very powerful tip, and exponentially more powerful when paired with the previous tip of how important it is to make the decision of how to position your product.

This is actually the second most important decision you must make in your advertising.

That is, what does your product promise to the customer?

Now, before you start thinking, let me tell you what a promise is NOT.

- A promise is NOT a claim.

- A promise is NOT a slogan.

- A promise is NOT a theme.

- A promise is a benefit for the consumer.

Additionally, if your benefit to the consumer is unique and competitive, that will be even better for your advertising.

Now, when you make a promise of a benefit, you must deliver or even over-deliver on your promises.

Your product MUST deliver on the promises of benefits that you advertise.

If you are able to achieve both efforts in making and delivering on a promise made in your advertising, you will be far ahead of others who are in your marketplace.

Tip #3 - Branding and Images

Think of some successful big companies that you know of and that are as well widely known.

Now think of their logo and branding image. Chances are, the ones you've picked you're able to immediately identify the business from the logo/branding. That is the power of having good branding images and logos.

However, when it comes to advertising, many people tend to make up branding images and logos as they go and never really take the time to create a branding image that can stand as a representation of what they are known by. Over 95% of all advertisement image is created this way.

Many companies fail to use a consistent image that they can be known by. By doing this, they will always lose marketplace position to the business that keeps a consistent image that it can be known for and in the same vein maintains and keeps its identity.

With that in mind, it makes sense for you to make a brand image that your business can be known by, so you can take a more dominant position in your marketplace over competitors.

Tip #4 - Big Ideas

Remember when you were a kid and someone probably told you to dream big? Well, in business and advertising it is very important for you to have a BIG Idea.

I mean, you could have a small idea, but who would want to take action or be moved to buy off of a small idea? Exactly. Probably nobody.

Unless your advertising is built on a BIG idea, it will simply fail.

I could go into telling you why, but I'm pretty sure you understand that small ideas won't work.

One thing to clarify before I go further on this is that a BIG idea does not mean a complicated idea. In fact, some of the most valuable (but hard to come by) ideas are the ones that make a big problem much simpler. It takes a BIG idea in order to get your customers to take action on what you've got.

For example, what if I said, "Hey, you should read my report and you might get a couple of sales."

You probably wouldn't even click on the report for one, and two, if you did read it with that in mind at the beginning you probably wouldn't get the massive value that this report is really worth!

On the other hand, what if I said, "Would it light a fire under you to read this entire report if I told you that the tips in it have led to millions of dollars in sales for many people and I'm giving them to you for free?!"

Now, while I'm sure that it does light a fire under you to read this report, I want you to know that your advertising must be built on a BIG idea in order to make a BIG impact in sales.

With that said, let's move on to the next tip before any of those people that have made millions start trying to wring my neck for giving you these tips for free!

Tip #5 - First Class Quality

In the previous tip, you read about how important it is to base your advertising on a BIG idea.

Another important thing to do is to present a first class kind of quality about your product.

Let me ask you this, "Would you rather eat at a restaurant that takes pride in keeping the place clean or a restaurant that has a cockroach infestation?" (and probably serves tasty food).

Now, if you're a normal human being and not a cockroach enthusiast, I'm sure that your pick would be the one that is kept clean. It's the same way with advertising. People will be more likely to buy from an advertisement that shows quality.

With your advertising, you want to make it have a first class look and image that you're proud to present. People don't like to buy when the advertisement is ugly.

In fact, if your advertisement is ugly then people will perceive your business that way and it will negatively affect your sales!

In other words, an ugly advertisement leads people to think your product is of lower quality and one they won't attempt to buy.

With that said, let the images that people see of your product be one that is of quality (and make sure you deliver on that quality!)

Tip #6 - Go the Distance

One of the common mistakes of many advertising campaigns is that they end up being far more complicated than they need to be.

In some cases, I understand that it may not yet be you that is making the decisions on how the advertising campaigns goes.

However, I will tell you that one of the main reasons that advertising campaigns for many companies becomes more complicated than necessary is because they are reflecting too many divergent views of too many executives.

Not only this, but companies as a whole have too long of a list of objectives they want to accomplish by incorporating them with their advertising.

The problem with this, is that it causes the company to never have a single simple promise that they can go the distance with and really create some massive wealth on it at the same time.

Remember from Tip #2 about having a big promise?

It will pay you much better to take a single promise the full distance rather than trying to take a bunch of a little here, and a little there only in little ways.

Of course, you may be thinking, "didn't you say that you know that some of us don't have a say in the advertising?"

I did say that and to that I say this, "It will pay you much better to take a single promise the full distance rather than trying to take a bunch of little ones only a little ways."

The reason I say it again is because for one it is important in advertising, but even also for you while you work for someone.

Even while you work for someone, what is your promise or benefit that you provide to the company?

Go the distance with that promise, so you can be given a better promise.

Of course, if you are already in charge of or part of the decision making, then this is an idea you cannot afford NOT to share with your company.

Tip #7 - Don't Be a Bore!

If you're still reading this at this point, then hopefully I haven't been boring you into reading this.

In fact, if you're still reading this, I sincerely hope that you have gotten massive value out of this report and you will waste no time starting to use these tips so you can build massive wealth in your business and take a more dominant position in your marketplace.

Of course, I hope you haven't skimmed and/or just skipped to this tip because you would find better, and more industry tested and trusted tips even better than this one!

With that said, applying this tip will most definitely make your customers appreciate you more!

All of these tips have been put together in order to provide you with massive values and to get your mind moving in the right directions when it comes to creating your advertising piece.

If you have massive value in what you're writing, then people will be interested in reading or hearing what you have to say. Not only that, but they'll share it with other people!

Anyhow, the final tip for today is that you do not want to bore your customers.

So have you ever been bored into buying?

I would think not, but how about this:

Have you ever bored anyone into buying?

I certainly hope not, but I know that I've seen some advertisements that seemed monotonous, cold, detached, plain, and impersonal.

Hopefully, that wasn't yours...

Anyhow, it is important to speak like a human being rather than your high school history teacher that read the text book in such a monotonous voice that it seemed like the clock was put to sleep!

Captivate your audience.

ABOUT THE AUTHOR

Audrey Woodley- a woman of power, charisma and influence; uses her platform to speak, teach, and coach women around the world.

Serving as a Motivational Speaker, Life Coach, and Brand Therapist; Audrey applies principles from her own life as a native of Chicago, Illinois, a single mother, a successful entrepreneur, and co-author of two International Best Selling Book to help women entrepreneurs reach success. Faith, she often tells her life coaching clients, is one of the most valuable tools and building blocks of any woman's success when applied persistently and consistently.

Audrey is best known as the Brand Therapist- in helping women identify solutions to brand challenges. She uses new-age problem solving tactics, proven social media strategies, effective marketing communication, and customized brand identity coaching. Audrey's own brand has seen great success including features in several magazines that focus on women entrepreneurial ventures and has been invited to speak at various functions including several workshops presented by Senator Kimberly Lightford. Audrey was a Emcee at the Walker's Legacy "Power 25" event, a Life Coach speaker for "Beauty For A Cause" event, and keynote speaker for Changing Oasis, Inc. events.

When it comes to speaking, coaching and consulting women entrepreneurs Audrey Woodley delivers!

.

Let's Get Social

Post Your review of The Beauty of Business... on Amazon & Kindle.
Captivate & Convert

Join the community at www.audreywoodley.com

and follow Audrey on Twitter (@ALWoodleyCEO)

Instagram (@AudreyWoodley), and LinkedIn

(https://www.linkedin.com/in/audreywoodley/).

The Beauty of Business Workshops

"Breakdown to Breakthrough", Conquer your fears and remove the boulders out of your way, and start living a purposeful life!

Audrey Woodley empowers women through workshops for women overcoming cancer and coaching for corporate, retreats, nonprofits. We also have special women groups to help women become self-empowered and live their authentic truth.

If you're interested in learning more about our joint venture book retreats, expo's, workshops, webinars, special events, speaking Or Transformational Coaching, then book Audrey to come speak at your group, organization, school, or book a consultation call bit.ly/B2BTherapy.

Please visit www.audreywoodley.com E:info@audreylwoodley.com

www.ingramcontent.com/pod-product-compliance
Lightning Source LLC
LaVergne TN
LVHW010032070426
835508LV00005B/301